Pretty Patty's First Day of School

Written by: Ava Johnson, M.A., PLPC

Professional Counselor, Therapist

Illustrated by: D. Artistic Touch

An 'Angelic Matters' Creation

ISBN: 978-0-578-71585-8

"Through Honesty, Awareness, & Acceptance, We Are Our Best."

- Ava Johnson, M.A., PLPC

Pretty Patty is very nervous, it's her first day of school.

As she awaits the bus, she has thoughts of children being cruel

Pointing and teasing about her mouth, making a grand ole fuss.

"Oh My Lord," Patty says, "I think I see the bus."

Having a cleft palate hasn't been a lot of fun.

Hospital visits and stares are what Patty's overcome.

Pretty Patty is sweating profusely, refusing to get on the bus.

"Mommy, mommy! Don't make me go," she said.

"Honey, hurry on and hush.

Pretty Patty you must go now.

The bus driver is in a rush," her Mommy said.

Pretty Patty picks a seat along for the ride.

She sat with fears, doubts, concerns, definitely less pride.

Scared that other children would tease her along the way,

a voice calls out from the back seat, "is this your first day?"

"Hi, my name is Jubilee.

I am quite unique as you can see.

I was born without a hand.

This one is T-i-t-a-n-i-u-m.

I even have a cute nickname.

I can show you, want to see?

They call me Judo Jubilee." She exclaimed.

Across the seat, the boy he smiled and entered into play.
"Hi, girls. My name is Mikey G., and it is my first day.

I have something special about me. In fact, it is my height.
It's no wonder why all my friends call me 'Big Mike.'"

The boy stood and turned around.
Wow, his stealth 6 feet off the ground.
The bus driver yells out, "young man sit down, sit down!"

The three new friends conversed the entire ride to school.
Pretty Patty thought to herself, "my new friends are cool."

Pretty Patty wasn't worried any longer what mean kids
would say.
So when a kid made fun of her,
she ignored him and went along her way.
Hurrying to her new class on her first day.

Pretty Patty sat in her seat as a lady entered the room.

Alas, Pretty Patty was surprised it was the lady from the hall.

She was sleek, beautiful, sophisticated, stood straight, and was tall.

There was one particular detail all noticed in the class.

This beautiful young lady was sporting a trim mustache.

"Hi, my name is A.B Snipp, but you can call me Counselor Snipp.

I will assume by all of the looks everyone has noticed the hair above

my lip. Now is a great time to discuss differences and respect.

No one will be cruel in our school is what I'll expect,"

she stated to the group.

Counselor Snipp's visit was very fun that day.

We participated in activities, ate candy, and also played.

Before we went home, she gave a little speech about being

kind to one another in the words that we speak.

"Children are majestical, parents give you special names.

They try to shield you from cruelty and that which brings you pain.

Every child is special. No two are the same.

All get their feelings hurt when spoken words of shame," she said.

Pretty Patty went to sleep that night in a peculiar state.

All was well now she understood being different was no mistake.

The beauty in the world is that we are all not alike.

Pretty Patty goes to sleep with confidence in her life.

The difference in her mouth was really no difference at all.

Like having a mustache, a special hand, or being really tall.

The End

Author Ava Johnson |

Ava J. Johnson is an Author from St. Louis, Mo. She is an expert in entrepreneurship, holding many titles in different business fields, including Co-Owner of Mi Hungry Catering and BBQ Jamaican Cuisine. Ms. Johnson is also a Licensed Social Worker, Consumer Directive Service Coordinator, Notary for the State of Missouri, International Traveler, and Socioculturalist.

"It's through my travels that I have learned that the human race, regardless of differences, share more in common than not," she stated. Further proving her compassionate stance on humans around the globe, she says, "you just have to take time to listen and relate," Ava says.

Throughout the years Ms. Johnson has shown her compassion for people to be true. Through countless donations and service hours in the communities she serves. She has mentored neighborhood youth, organized community volunteer days for inner city youth, encouraged good grades to children with quarterly incentives, and providing keynote speeches.

"Ava gave one of the most phenomenal motivational speeches in the history of the Human Service Program."- Dr. Howard Rosenthal, Director of Human Service Program at Florissant Valley Community College (October 24, 2016)

Ms. Johnson is a true humanitarian, entrepreneur, socialist with experiences to inspire and motivate the masses. She is available for book tours, keynote speeches and presentations pertaining to entrepreneurship, teen parenting, human services, education, and youth related topics.

She can be reached for bookings at: mommie.mihungry@gmail.com

What can you do if you are being bullied?

Coping with bullying can be difficult, but always remember the bully is the problem not you! You have the right to be safe.

Talk to a Trusted Adult

Many kids and teens who are targeted by bullies, feel embarrassed or ashamed. By discussing the situation with an adult you will not feel alone. An adult can help you develop a plan to end the bullying.

Act Confident

Hold your head up, stand up straight, make eye contact, and walk confidently. A bully is less likely to single you out if you appear confident.

Try to Make Other Friends

A bully is more likely to leave you alone if you are with your friends.

What can you do to help someone being bullied?

Tell an Adult in Charge

Talking to a school counselor, teacher, principal, and even your parents, can bring attention to the problem. Tell the adult how long you have witnessed the bullying occurring and in detail an example.

Move Closer to the Person Being Bullied

By moving closer to the person being bullied, you make the person feel like he/she are not alone.

Be Kind and Speak

Simply saying hello and being kind is a way to lift the spirits of someone the target of bullying.

Invite Person Being Bullied into Your Group

Making new friends and being invited in activities, helps the person being bullied understand that the bully is the problem not her/him.

National Bullying Prevention
Hotline
1.866.488.7386

National Bullying Prevention
Month
October

www.ingramcontent.com/pod-product-compliance
Lightning Source LLC
Chambersburg PA
CBHW040347060426
42445CB00029B/39